Contents

INTRODUCTION

Adding a water garden is a major undertaking, but it may well be one of the best and most pleasurable garden additions you will ever make. Take the time now—before you ever lift a spade—to thoughtfully design and plan your water garden.

Doing your homework now saves frustrations and disappointment later. Learn about the best place to locate a water feature, the most fitting style, and the latest design and building techniques. The result will be a water feature that installs easily, requires minimal fuss, and is a focal point of your landscape for years to come. It's equally important that your water garden match your lifestyle and your goals for it. Will it be a private retreat or a place to entertain guests? Will you enjoy it mainly during the day or evening? Do you have the time and desire to putter with extensive plantings and fish, or do you want something low-maintenance?

CHAPTER ONE

What Kind of Water Feature Is Right For You?

Give some thought to the kind of personality you want your water garden to have. Ideally it should harmonize not only with your home's architecture, but also the character of the rest of your property.

To arrive at a design, start with thinking about formal and informal styles, or create your own design that is a hybrid of the two. Also draw inspiration from water gardens You have seen in person or in photos. Many approaches and styles have been used throughout history and still have an influence today— Moorish, Italian, French, Japanese, and others. Envision the flat, glassy planes of water at Tuscany's Villa Gamberaia. Or think of the lush natural look of Monet's water garden in France. Have fun and dream big dreams!

Formal water gardens are usually based on a symmetrical shape: a square, rectangle, or perfect circle or oval. Depending on how they're designed, they fit in with equally formal surroundings or a landscape that's quite informal.

A formal water garden can be a good choice for a smaller garden. Think of the little courtyards with fountains in Spain and Mexico. Large, expansive properties can also be compatible with a formal-style display. With some formal water gardens, there is an emphasis on the reflections off the water surface. Many include a fountain or statuary. Formal pools and ponds also usually use regular, neat edging materials, such as bricks, blocks, and tiles. "Monoculture" plantings of just one plant, such as water lilies, are popular in formal water gardens. So are monochromatic planting schemes, using only white flowers, for instance.

Informal garden pools are more casual in shape and more versatile for planting schemes of all kinds. Pools in various irregular shapes, such as kidney, teardrop, lagoon, and "amoeba," are just a few of the ones you can either buy pre-formed or create with flexible line.

To give your informal garden that desirable "settled" look, take a cue from nature. Ponds in nature range from plants floating in deeper water, to plants growing in shallow water, to plants growing on the banks. This transitional effect is easy to imitate. Place plants on your pool's side shelves (pre-formed liners often come with these shelves), or raise them up on a support. Then grow moisture-loving plants alongside your pool. Go for a combination of plants that includes various colors, leaf forms, and textures. Water lilies and other aquatic plants that float or trail on the water's surface can be offset nicely by what professional landscape designers call "vertical accents" in the form of tall marginal plants. The combination lends your feature variety and interest.

A Water Garden Is an Ecosystem

A healthy water garden has clear water, active fish, and thriving plants. It smells and even feels in tip-top shape.

Fish do their part by eating mosquitoes and nibbling plants. Floating plants shade the water, preventing the growth of algae and keeping it cool and clear for fish. Marginal and submerged plants provide more cover for fish and other wildlife, and also filter impurities out of the water. A fountain aerates the water, keeping it oxygenated for fish. Filters catch particles in the water and prevent bacterial problems. A skimmer keeps debris off the surface of the water, and if you want, you can add filters inside the skimmer.

Every water garden needs different types of bacteria to keep the water healthy. Some bacteria foul the water, but others help keep it clear by breaking down debris and waste. One helpful type is nitrifying bacteria, which convert harmful ammonia from fish waste into less harmful nitrite and then nitrate—which is taken up in small quantities by plants as fertilizer.

The type of filter you choose can promote healthy bacterial growth. Some contain plastic balls, rocks, or media on which the bacteria are contained and continue to thrive.

Plants also play a vital role. Plant roots take up pollutants in the water, such as fish waste, use them as fuel for growth, then filter them and release oxygen into the water and air. Submerged plants are especially good at this because their many leaves are underwater, releasing oxygen directly into the water.

Floating plants are helpful too. They shade the water, greatly reducing the growth of algae, which needs sun to thrive. Floating plants also provide shade for fish so they don't overheat, and cover from overhead predators, such as birds or raccoons.

The Role of Pumps and Filters

In nature, water is filtered and aerated by running through layers of stone or moving along a streambed. In the artificial environment of a home garden, you must mimic this process with pumps and filters. These important pieces of equipment move water so that oxygen is incorporated into the water from the air. Well- oxygenated water prevents the growth of anaerobic bacteria, those bacteria that make stagnant water smell bad and feel slimy.

There are many different pumps and filters to choose from, depending on the size of your water feature and the various options you desire. Even a tiny container garden does much better with a small pump and fountain to keep the water fresh. Smaller gardens need at least one good mechanical filter, while larger gardens need more complex filters and more powerful pumps to move the greater volume of water. Mechanical filters must be rinsed every few days or so, especially in warmer weather. Still other filters contain beneficial bacteria and others zap organisms with UV rays.

Understanding Liners

Pre-formed Rigid Liners

Rigid liners are highly popular and can last a long time (though not forever). It is wise to invest in quality materials in order to get maximum mileage.

In particular, seek out good UV resistance because exposure to sunlight weakens plastic and causes it to crack and leak over time. When shopping for a pre-formed pool liner, you will find plenty of choices. They tend to be strong, rigid black plastic or, less commonly, fiberglass. You may see ones with full or partial shelves, ones with stream configurations or waterfall lips, round ones, kidney-shaped ones, teardrops, and so on. They can be 2, 3, or even 5 feet across and 6 feet long or longer. It would seem that installing a rigid liner would be easier than a flexible liner. However, especially if you have a complex shape with multiple levels, it can be difficult to dig the hole to conform perfectly. It is important to dig away as little soil as possible so there is a minimum of settling once the liner is in position. You must also backfill in very precisely to support marginal shelves and the weight of the water. Otherwise, settling—a common problem with rigid liners—may occur.

With all liners, it's important to get the liner level, but this is especially true with rigid liner. If the rigid liner isn't perfectly level, it will be very apparent since the water will slope unevenly from one side to the other.

Flexible Liners

Flexible liners allow you to create a pond or stream of just about any size or shape. It's easier to completely conceal flexible liners than it is rigid liners because you can wrap and shape edges precisely the way you want to work with the edging you choose. Choose liner made specifically for ponds. They hold up to the special conditions of a water garden, including UV light, and are fish-safe. Professional water garden designers recommend the three following types of flexible liner, purchased separately or as part of a kit.

- **45-mil EPDM rubber**

EPDM stands for ethylene propylene diene monomer. Considered the liner of choice for most jobs, it is extremely durable and puncture resistant. It is also extremely flexible, which is handy when trying to tuck and turn and twist liner into irregular shapes. This is especially important in a small pond, where you'll have to tuck and fold the liner a lot to fit into the small hole.

However, size is a limitation if you are doing a very large job. The largest roll size manufactured is 50 feet by 100 feet, and seaming two pieces of EPDM rubber is tricky. It is done on the site where you're installing your pond and requires the right temperature and humidity levels, a flat solid foundation to work on, and messy seam tape.

• 40-mil polypropylene

If your pond requires a liner larger than the 50 feet by 100 feet available for EPDM rubber, consider 40-mil polypropylene. It's actually more durable and puncture-resistant than 45- mil EPDM, but it's not nearly as flexible, so it is harder to conform to various holes and shapes.

• 30-mil polyethylene

Least expensive of liners, it costs about half of polypropylene and EPDM rubber. It's stiff and can be difficult to work with. It does not hold up well to the beating it takes from the placement of large stone, so you must be especially careful with it. And for large projects, it can't be seamed without expensive welding equipment, usually by a professional.

Understanding Pumps

Pumps are critical to a successful water garden. They power waterfalls, pull water through filters, and spray water from fountains.

Pumps come in a variety of sizes and styles, and can be combined with other features of a water garden. A small pump for a container water garden may have a filter and fountainhead built right in. Another medium-sized pump may have a foam-type filter attached, or should be placed in a filter box. Adequate power is key. Too little power and the pump creates a weak, unappealing waterfall or fountain, or hinders filters and skimmers from working well.

With pumps, you get what you pay for: durability and power. The smallest pumps for tabletop versions. A pump large enough to power a nice bubbler fountainhead in a pool maybe the size of a large bathtub. And a pump that will turn over the volume of a medium-sized pond, power a fountainhead, a pressure-fed filter, and a waterfall

2 or 3 feet high. The key number to know in choosing a pump is gallons per hour. You need a pump powerful enough to turn over the entire volume of your pond, stream, or waterfall at least once every hour. So a 300-gallon pond needs a 300 or more

GPH pump.

When in doubt, buy a more powerful pump (perhaps 25 to 50 percent more than you think you need). You can restrict the flow—most pumps have valves to adjust this—but you can't add power needs. GPH needs can be surprisingly high. If you are building an 8-foot by 4-foot pond, 2 feet deep, with a 15-foot stream attached, topped by a waterfall that rises 2 feet, you will need a pump with a 1,200-1,500 GPH.

Additional GPH for waterfalls: Besides the number of gallons in your water feature, you also need to know how much additional GPH your pump will need to achieve lift for any waterfall. The easiest way to determine this is to look at pump package/label information. Most will tell you how much GPH the pump provides for various heights and numbers of waterfalls.

Additional GPH for tubing: If you are using tubing to run from the pump to a waterfall or other feature, add in about another foot of lift (check the package) for every 10 feet of tubing.

Additional GPH for a more generous flow of water over falls, especially wide waterfalls: Use this rough rule of thumb—for a 1-inch thick sheet of water 1 inch wide over a waterfall, add 150 GPH to the pump. For 1 inch of water flowing 6 inches across, add 900 GPH.

Water gardens are seldom neat, regular, geometric shapes that make it easy to calculate the overall volume of the water. So figuring out the volume—and therefore determining a key number in choosing a pump—is tricky. You can do some general estimating by taking simple measurements. With a pond that is a roughly oval abstract shape, measure how long it is, how wide, and how deep in the deepest part and then calculate it the same way you would a rectangular box. You can also figure out how wide, on average, a stream is and how deep it will be. Then calculate the number of cubic feet of water. Convert cubic feet into gallons by multiplying by 7.48.

This method give you more gallons than the actual amount, but within reason that's okay because your pump should be powerful enough to turn over at least the total volume of water every hour. There are several helpful online calculators for figuring out how many gallons of water your water feature will contain and the GPH needed.

Understanding and Choosing Filters

• Mechanical Filters

A mechanical filter is basically a very good strainer. Water runs through it, pushed or pulled by a pump. Foam, netting, grates, or screening catches particles in the water. Mechanical filters need regular rinsing out, usually every few to several days. This usually consists of lifting out the filter and giving it a hard spray with a hose for a minute or two.

• Prefilters

A prefilter is simply a type of filter that prevents particles from clogging a pump right before they are sucked into the pump. Prefilters come in several different styles, such as a piece of foam that fits on the end of or around a portion of the pump or a removable device encased in plastic attached with a slatted snap-on encasement. Or the prefilter can be a separate mechanism alongside the pump, attached with tubing.

• Biological Filters

A biological filter is basically a housing that provides the necessary habitat for beneficial bacterial colonization. Like mechanical filters, biological filters come in many different styles. Most, however consist of a media of plastic, rock, or ceramic on which helpful bacteria live. Biological filters may also contain enzymes. The water is pulled or pushed through the biological filter usually with the help of a pump. The water flows into the filter, over the media and the beneficial bacteria, and then back out into the pond. The water must be pumped constantly or the helpful bacteria can die. As with mechanical filters, you must clean biological filters occasionally—anywhere from every month or so to once a year. Shown at right is a bag of biomedia balls, which rest in a biofalls setup, getting a good hosing.

• UV Filters or Clarifiers

These expose water to ultraviolet light to kill problem-causing single-celled organisms, such as algae, fish parasites, and non-beneficial bacteria.

Water is pulled or pushed with a pump into a container equipped with an ultraviolet light bulb. The organisms that pass through and are pumped out with the water are exposed to the UV light, their DNA is altered, and they eventually die. It's an effective method for controlling floating algae. UV clarifiers are discouraged by some water gardening professionals. They would rather see gardeners making sure their garden is in ecological balance and avoid UV clarifiers because they disagree with the assertion that the UV rays don't also kill beneficial bacteria and microorganisms along with the bad.

UV clarifiers are available housed in tubelike casing, or they can be a part of other types of filters in boxes. Still others are designed for mounting outside the pond. The one shown here is designed to be buried almost up to its top alongside the pond with water flowing through tubing connected to a pump.

Skimmer

This is basically a large box with an opening on the top of one side, positioned just below the surface of the water, off to one side of the water feature. Floating debris such as leaves and sticks flow into an inlet that looks like a window, level with water surface. The water flows into a box or net that catches leaves, twigs, debris, dust, pollen, and more and then is pumped out back into the pond. The skimmer box or net must be emptied periodically, depending on the site, the feature, and the time of year.

Skimmers are almost essential with large streams, since the stream and any waterfalls are open to a large area and therefore can catch a large amount of debris. Also, if the pump in a stream or waterfall gets clogged, it can stop the whole water feature from functioning. A skimmer prevents this.

Biofalls

The large pre-formed black plastic waterfall lips— also called weirs or header pools—often also contain some form of filtration. These filters may include sheets of foam, mesh bags of lava rock or bioballs, or other combination mechanical/ biological filters. Some water gardeners even report success using special barley treatments in biofalls. Like all filters, biofalls must be cleaned out from time to time. Most need to be cleaned once a year. The pre-formed waterfall here usually has media, such as a bag of bioballs, or foam-type filter mats to filter the water that flows through from the bottom and up over the top of the lip.

Understanding Edging

Edging is essential to a water feature's good looks— helping it blend into its surrounding and hiding the less-attractive liners but it also does so much more: Edging holds the liner in place. And when well installed, it helps protect the liner from destructive UV rays from the sun. It can help prevent soil and debris from washing into the water garden.

Types of Edging

When deciding on an edging material, take into account other materials already in your hardscape.

If there's a lot of brick, consider that material. If there's already naturalistic flagstone, try some more of that. Mix and match stones carefully. Limestone and granite together can look jarring, unless very carefully done. Also even the same type of stone, such as limestone, can have very different coloring. Buy all your stone in one group, if you can.

Materials for edging include:

• Flagstones

• Cut stone

• Rounded boulders of all sizes

• Brick

• Pavers

• A combination of boulders and smaller stones and gravel

CHAPTER TWO

PONDLESS WATERFALL

A pondless waterfall is the perfect solution for small spaces or homes with young children. It's also a great feature for a front yard because it can fit in easily to a corner or near the front door. With a pondless waterfall, water is held in a reservoir (also called a basin) at the bottom of the falls. The basin is filled with stones, gravel, or hollow crate-like boxes that are covered with stones.

Water in the reservoir is pumped out by a pump (the cord runs off to the side to an outdoor power source). The pump propels the water through black plastic tubing up to the head of the waterfall. Gravity forces it to flow downward back into the gravel bed and the cycle begins all over again. Keep in mind that the reservoir must have enough capacity to hold all the water should the pump fail and water suddenly rush downward into the pool.

Key design points include:

• Most basins at the bottom are not more than a couple feet deep.

• The pump often is set into a special, deeper hole just large enough to hold it to assure that it will always be surrounded with water even when water levels get low.

Pools or Ponds

Highly formal or very natural looking, pools and ponds are simply any portion of a water garden that allows water to collect in a pool. They can be rigid liner or flexible, aboveground or below. Many pools are combined with waterfalls, streams, or different types of fountains.

Waterfalls

The charming splashing sound of a waterfall offers appeal for nearly any home. A waterfall can be a foot high or many feet high. It can be attached to a pool or pond or can be part of a stream. All waterfalls need pools at the bottom, but some have buried pools or reservoirs hidden from sight or have no visible pool or pond at all. Waterfalls can have one simple cascade or multiple cascades delivered from a hidden manifold, over multiple rocks or lips. Create your own waterfall with stone or other materials, or use pre-formed weirs or waterfall forms. Waterfalls work with both rigid and flexible liners, depending on your design.

How Large Should Your Water Feature Be?

Very few first-time water gardeners regret making a water feature too big. Rather, they find that they wish they had made it larger so they could have gotten even more pleasure out of it. Also, a medium-sized water feature usually takes about the same time and effort to care for as a smaller one. Cost is a factor, and the larger the water feature, the higher the cost.

And if you are doing it yourself, you will need to calculate how much time and skill it will take to build and maintain. Generally, smaller water features do take less skill and expertise than very large water features.

How Big Is Big?

Small water features, such as fountains and pools not much bigger than a luxury soaker bathtub, are great because they're easier to construct and maintain. They're also ideal for first-time water gardeners to quite literally get their feet wet and learn about the mechanics and care involved in a water garden.

Medium-sized water gardens have a surface of perhaps 10 feet by 10 feet. Larger water gardens can take at least an hour of care a week and can be complicated to design and build, but they are more dramatic and can transform a landscape. Whatever size water garden you're planning, it is important to know its volume. This will help you determine everything from pump power to how much of a pond product, such as an algaecide, to use.

Sizing for Fish

If you want to have fish of any size or number, you will need a certain minimum depth and size. It is important to have enough water to support fish or the conditions will become unhealthy with too much fish waste and too much competition for oxygen. To calculate the maximum size and number of fish you should have in your pond, figure the total surface area of the water feature. Allow for 1 inch of fish for each 6 to 12 square inches of water. For koi, however, double that— for 1 inch of koi allow for at least 12 square inches of surface and preferably 24 square inches.

If you live in an area with severe winters, and you want to overwinter fish or plants in your pond, you'll need to size your pond accordingly. Larger ponds are less likely to freeze than small ones.

If a pond contains 100 gallons, in places where temperatures don't often dip below -20°F, it probably won't freeze. In colder zones, the pond needs at least 500 gallons to assure fluid water at the bottom of the pond in severe cold.

To prevent the pond from freezing solid, it needs a deep zone.

• In areas with lows of -10°F, the deep zone should be 20 inches.

• In areas with lows of -20°F, the deep zone should be 24 inches.

• In areas with lows of -30°F, if you want to be really safe, the deep zone could be as deep as

30 inches.

Understanding Electrical Elements

Electricity is needed to power pumps, waterfalls, pond heaters, filters, and in some cases runs lighting. It is also useful to have on hand in using power equipment around your water feature.

Most water features run on a standard 120- volt household current. A very large feature might need a 220-volt dedicated circuit, the type used for major household appliances such as clothes dryers or air conditioners.

GFCI outlets

Ground-Fault Circuit Interrupter (GFCI) outlets are a critical safety feature for any outdoor electrical use. You'll see them in bathrooms and kitchens where water is used, and they have a little reset (usually red) button in the center.

The GFCI senses any electrical contact with water as well as any overload, and instantly stops the current, preventing bad shocks and even electrocution. Any power outlet installed outdoors these days must be GFCI. If you live in an older home, you may come across some ungrounded outlets, but do not use them for a water feature. If you have a GFCI outlet within 6 to 10 or so feet (the length of most water feature electrical cords) of where you want your water garden, you are set.

Otherwise, you'll need to have one installed. (If you use an extension cord, make sure that it is rated for external use.) GFCI boxes can be mounted on fence posts or other permanent objects, or installed freestanding just a few inches above the ground, hidden behind plants. Although an experienced amateur can often install this, local electrical codes may require a licensed professional.

Working with Foam

Waterfall foam comes in a pressurized can and, like insulation foam, expands when released. It anchors stones in place, and fills voids between the rocks and liner, diverting water around and over stones. It's far easier to use than mortar and won't crack in freezing temperatures. And while the goal is for it to be completely covered with stonework, its black color blends in, looking like stone or shadow. When dry, if necessary, it can be peeled or cut or trimmed away—much like soft Styrofoam— but this is a last resort. There's a skill to using waterfall foam.

<u>**Some tips for best results:**</u>

• Because of its quickly expanding nature, waterfall foam can be a little hard to control until you get the hang of it. If you've never used it before, experiment with it a bit first before working on your actual project.

• Wear disposable gloves. It sticks to skin and can be nearly impossible to get out from underneath nails. (Use a pumice stone to remove any that gets on your skin.)

• For small projects, working directly from a one-time use can is fine. However, for larger projects, invest in a foam gun with a long pin-point barrel. It allows you to work more precisely between stones and allows instant shut-off of the foam. (Also invest in foam gun cleaner!)

• Foam adheres better to damp surfaces than dry. Moisten (but don't soak) stones and liner beforehand for ideal contact.

• With larger stones and boulders, apply a thin layer of black foam underneath and on the sides of each stone. Use only a thin coat because the foam will expand.

Understanding Lighting

Almost every water garden needs some lighting or another. After all, lights and water are a magical combination that plays off each other beautifully.

Also, unlike the regular garden, a water feature sometimes is best enjoyed at night because of the lights. And it's also cooler and quieter at night, making for a more relaxing experience. Some water garden lighting operates off a standard 120-volt household current. This type of lighting usually requires considerable electrical experience or even a licensed electrician to install. However, the popularity of low-voltage lighting has exploded in the past few years and for good reason—it's easy to install yourself. When thinking about adding lighting to your water feature, be aware of the different types:

Floating

Floating lights drift atop the water, like little floating luminarias. They are anchored at the bottom of the pool or pond with anchors supplied with the lights. Some are simple and elegant, such as frosted white globes, and others are novelties, such as illuminated lily pads.

Submerged

Submerged lights can be used in several ways. Available both as floodlights and spotlights, they are—as the name suggests—installed under the water. Often a spotlight is beamed up out of the water to highlight a statue or dramatic plant. Submerged lights can also be put under fountains or waterfalls and shone upward to make the moving water appear to glow.

• Floodlight

Floodlights can be used in water or outside the water feature. On dry land, they are excellent for lighting a large area, such as a seating area. Or they can be used as uplights underneath a large feature, such as a tree, with the extra light illuminating the whole area. In the water, they can be used to illuminate an entire pool. Just be sure to direct the beam away from where people will be observing the pool, or it might create glare.

• Spotlight

Spotlights also can be used in or out of the water. Use them to shine upward to highlight a statue or a tree, but unlike a floodlight, there will be less scattered light to illuminate the whole area.

Fountain Spray Lights

Among the showiest of water feature lighting, pond jets (also called fountain spray lights) dramatically illuminate a fountain. Choose from white or other colors. These floating lights are sold in sets of three or more or in a kit, often with a submersible pump and a timer, which work in tandem with the lights themselves.

Landscape Lights

Regular lighting in the garden can also be used around the water feature. Footlights are wonderful surrounding a pond or stream edge. They are also useful to provide safety and beauty along porches, paths, and decks near water features.

Low-Voltage Lighting

Unlike regular electrical features, low-voltage systems are safe and easy for even beginners to install Tiered lights, also called pagoda lights, are widely available and the most popular type of low-voltage light. They provide downlight along paths and driveways and are striking when surrounding a pool or pond. Low-voltage lights also are available as spotlights and floodlights. They are also available as submerged lighting and floating lighting. Light-emiting diode (LED) bulbs are highly efficient and last a decade or more. They cost more, but pay for themselves in energy efficiency.

Building Your Water Feature

Follow these tips to dig smart, saving your back and your time.

• A few days before you plan to excavate, dig an "exploratory" hole or two a couple feet wide and as deep as your water garden. This will let you determine if there are many rocks, clay, hardpan, or roots and allow you to plan accordingly.

• If the area has lots of roots, keep a mattock, a long-handled lopper, and a small saw on hand to work through the roots.

• In areas with hardpan or clay, soak the area thoroughly the day before with water to soften the clay. If the soil is very dry, you may need to water twice in two days.

• In clay soils, use a fiberglass-handled roundpoint shovel—it won't break as easily. In severe clay hardpan, try a pick axe.

• Hoist large rocks out with a long-handled pry bar and remove them with the help of a friend. If you hit one that's immovable, consider designing around it (easy to do with flexible liner).

• For larger projects, consider renting a backhoe or ditch digger. Rentals are usually reasonably priced.

Tools and Supplies

Round-point shovel

Flat-edged shovel

Wheelbarrow

Tarp (optional)

Trowel

Pick-axe (for hardpan or dry clay soils)

Rented jackhammer (for rocky or severe

hardpan soils)

Heavy work gloves

Heavy work boots

Outline

Use spray paint or a garden hose or stakes and twine to mark the outline. Keep spray paint on hand since you'll be using it for any additional layers to be added to the pool.

• Start Excavating

If you are creating shelves and different depths, dig out the first layer of soil of the water garden, that is, the overall shape down to the first ledge.

• Check the level as you work.

Pile soil on a driveway, patio, or on a tarp on the lawn.

Repeat the marking process for the second and any third level of the water garden, mark where the shelves or ledges should be. As needed, use a flat-edged shovel or hand trowel to shape the ledge. They are more precise than a round-point shovel. Check the level again.

Tips for a Perfect Level

Getting your water garden excavated with perfect level is critical. Water always seeks to be level, so if you dig one end a little deeper or higher than the other, it will be painfully apparent once you fill the feature with water. This is especially true with a rigid liner, formal pond, or highly regular edging (such as brick). With flexible liner, if things are a little off, you can cover up mistakes to some minor degree with artfully placed stone and gravel. But with a rigid liner, that is not usually possible.

Follow these tips to achieve perfect level every time:

• Use the right level for the job. That 8-inchlong level you use around the house for small projects just won't cut it. The longer the level, the more precise it is over a distance. For a water garden project, use a 48-inch-long level. Then set the level on a perfectly straight piece of lumber, stretched across the pool, pond, or streambed.

• For large projects, you can stretch string straight across, taut, and use a line level or hold the level along the string. But this technique has limited precision. For a more accurate (and easier) reading of level, invest in a laser level.

• Take your time. Getting level is important. You may need to backfill or redo—but it will be time well spent. If you're installing a rigid liner, be prepared to remove it as many times as needed to get it perfectly straight.

• Check level throughout the project. Be meticulous and check frequently while digging and each time you seat items such as a skimmer or pre-formed waterfall unit.

• As you work, tamp down sand and soil evenly. The weight of the water and any stones can settle soil by as much as an inch or two. Tamp down firmly and evenly to make sure your water feature isn't level when you install it but then settles unevenly and is no longer level.

Disposing off Leftover Soil

Soil from excavation can be used to level the area around the water feature or to build a grade for a stream or waterfall. Otherwise, good-quality topsoil can be spread elsewhere in the landscape, especially into raised beds and berms.

Subsoil (the lesser-quality soil underneath the topsoil that is usually laden with clay) or other problem soils aren't suitable for growing things, so you'll need to dispose of it. As you dig, pile the soil on the driveway or other paved area or on a tarp spread out on the grass (remove the tarp in a day or two or you'll kill the grass).

Waste disposal services sometimes will provide a special oversized dumpsterlike box into which you can load the excess dirt that they'll haul away. Or check want ads or online for "fill dirt"—someone may take it from you for no charge to use in construction projects. Otherwise, contact an excavation, contractor, or landscaping company about hauling it away for a fee.

How to Install a Flexible Liner

Once you've dug the hole, now comes the easy part: installing the flexible liner. For any water feature more than a few yards across, it's good to have a helper or even two or three to help with this process. Liner is surprisingly heavy—a 10 by 20 piece weighs about 80 pounds! And, as with making a big bed, it's useful to have someone on the other side, helping to arrange things so you don't have to walk several feet for every tweak and tug.

Flexible liner is more pliable in warm conditions, so try to time your project for a sunny day that is at least 65° F. Spread out the liner, as much as space permits, and allow it to warm in the sun for an hour or two.

Position the Underlayment

Use an underlayment made specifically for water gardens to prevent punctures and tears in the liner itself. Position the underlayment as precisely as you can into the water garden.

Position the Liner

Spread the liner over the underlayment, smoothing any wrinkles. If seams are necessary, follow the seaming instructions recommended for that type of liner. Different liners require different techniques, but most suggest overlapping the pieces by 18 inches and sealing with a compatible double-sided EPDM joint tape.

Weight the liner with stones to hold it in place as you work to position it. Where practical, add an inch or two of water to the bottom to help it settle more firmly into the hole.

Tools and Supplies

• Heavy-duty scissors

• Garden hose attached to spigot

• Flexible liner

• Underlayment

Add Accessories

Position any accessories that affect the liner, such as skimmer boxes or premade waterfall forms. Connect the liner to these following instructions from the manufacturer of each accessory.

Most recommend using an aquariumgrade silicone sealant on all joints and fastening parts with corrosion-resistant fasteners (such as stainless steel) to avoid leaks.

Trim the liner, leaving a 2-foot margin along the edges.

Position Gravel, Stones, and Edging

As much as is practical, cover the liner with a layer of washed stones and gravel to protect it from punctures and the destructive UV rays of the sun. Add more water if practical.

Add other stones and edging before making any final trims to the liner.

How to Install a Rigid Liner Pond

A rigid liner is appealing to many just getting started in water gardening. It's simple to wrap your brain around design and installation, and therefore most liners are small, targeted at beginning water gardens.

However, rigid liners are not without their drawbacks. Getting them (and keeping them) level over the years can be challenging. Also, if you want a natural look, the rigid edge is tricky to conceal.

But for many first-time water gardeners, rigid liners are the perfect way to truly dip their toes into the world of water gardening.

Outline the Pond

Using the level or another straight-edged tool, mark the edge of the liner on the ground with a rope.

Dig the Pond

Cut away any existing sod and reuse as desired. Measure the depth of the liner at the center and excavate the base to that depth. Dig the hole 2″ to 3″ deeper than the liner and past the edges of the outline by a couple of inches. Match the contours of the liner as closely as possible so the marginal shelves will be supported by soil and sand.

Position the Liner

Remove any rocks or roots and cover the bottom with 1 to 2 inches of sand. Set the liner in place to see how well it fits and adjust the sand on the underside until the liner rim is slightly above the

Test, level, and adjust. Be sure to use ample sand so no settling occurs. Also, be sure the level is exact. Water always is level, so if the liner is positioned even slightly off, it will be obvious.

If the pond is small, you may want to double-check the level by filling partly or fully with water. Empty the pond by at least half by bailing with a bucket as much as you can and proceed. (Some water will help anchor the pond.)

Tamp in the Soil and Sand

Fill in around the sides with a mixture of soil and sand. Use a trowel and hands to pack it in firmly, dampening with water as you go to further settle the sand.

If you are adding edging and compactable gravel, leave room for those elements.

Adding Edging Stones

Stones, concrete pavers, or other edging may be added for a decorative touch or to disguise the lip of the liner.

This edging is being placed on top of a layer of compactable gravel to hold them more steadily than sand and soil would. Layer the gravel 1 to 2 inches deep, and then tamp down firmly. Using a tamping tool is ideal.

Edging can be just one course (layer) or two, overlapping as desired to further disguise the lip. However, the stone must not press down heavily on the lip or it can damage it.

How to Build a Waterfall

Calculating the type of pump and head and lift needed for a waterfall is science. But laying the stone for a waterfall is art.

A pre-formed waterfall unit can take out a lot of the guesswork. But when it comes to regulating water flow—especially upstream and adjusting stones and rocks so that the water splashes over them just right—it's a matter of working with the shape and size of the rocks for the effect that is most pleasing to you.

Anatomy of a Waterfall

A pre-made waterfall unit holds a reservoir of water and creates a solid base on which to position stones. The spill stone is the stone that the water flows over, supported underneath by the foundation stone. A foundation stone supports the spill stone, usually along the front of the waterfall unit.

Tips For Building the Perfect Waterfall

Consider the terrain. If your backyard is flat, a waterfall that pops up out of nowhere will not look natural. If necessary, modify the terrain somewhat by building a berm a few feet high. For the most natural look with a waterfall, create several smaller drops of 4 to 9 inches or one drop of no more than 18 inches.

Proportion stones with the drop of the waterfall in mind. The main rocks along the side of the waterfall boulders should be a few to several inches larger than the drop of the waterfall. For example, for a drop of 12 inches, you should use rocks that are 16 inches across.

Use gate stones. Use some of the largest stones in the project to frame the waterfall. These stones channel the water to the waterfall, over the waterfall, and then can keep it in check as it flows farther down.

Go fewer and bigger. Fewer rocks are better when building a waterfall. Three large stones are better than 12 small stones stacked up. In nature, you usually find one very large stone, surrounded by few smaller ones, with the water running between them.

Design twists and turns. Create these in the waterfall and stream so that there are new views and facets with every turn. They also improve sound.

Add plants. The more plant material you use to line the falls and stream, the better. They soften raw, hard edges and make the waterfall look like it has always been there.

• Start with a Pre-formed Waterfall Unit

You can build a waterfall without one, but these make the job much easier by giving you a solid base structure and built-in reservoir. Position it at the top of the waterfall or stream. Bonus: You can put filters inside of the reservoir to make the unit do double duty.

• Lay the Liner

Position the flexible liner along the stream, attaching it to the waterfall unit as directed by the unit manufacturer. Aquarium-grade silicone is usually recommended as a sealant. Seal pieces as needed, following the liner manufacturer's instructions, but usually with EPDM tape and 18-inch overlap. Position any seams under a waterfall so that the top piece overlaps the bottom piece.

• Start Positioning the Stones

Put the foundation stones in place first, using mortar or expandable waterfall foam. (Have smaller stones nearby to set into any waterfall foam that shows.) Top with the spill stone and then position with various gate stones.

• Fill In With Smaller Stones

Use cobblestones and other small stones strategically to disguise the foam holding the larger stones in place.

• Add Gravel and More Stones

Cover the liner with washed gravel and cobblestones.

Fish and Plants

Creating a water garden opens up a new world filled with fascinating plants with growth habits that may be completely new to you. Some have gorgeous flowers; some have attractive, variegated, or intriguing foliage; and some have all—there are many appealing choices.

Water gardening also gives you an opportunity to keep fish. Fabulously colored, ever moving, surprisingly interactive, fish are the living jewels of a water garden. They're simple to keep, but pay off big, eliciting cries of delight from children and adults alike who spot them from under the cover of water lilies. Larger fish, especially the ornamental carp known as koi, can even be trained to eat out of your outstretched hand.

Water Quality for Fish and Plants

If your water feature contains no plants or fish, your primary water quality concern is simple: keeping algae at bay. If you want to include fish, you'll need to give some thought to water quality. While fish will tolerate many different types of water, for them to be in tip-top health, it is smart for you to take into account everything from chloramines to nitrogen levels.

• The Right pH Levels

You may already be familiar with pH in your garden soil since some plants prefer acidic soil and some prefer alkaline. The pH level describes how alkaline (also called basic or hard) or how acidic the water is, measured on a 14-point scale. With both soil and water, a pH of 7 is considered neutral. A pH higher than 7 is basic while levels below 7 are acidic.

Typical, healthy ponds have a pH range from 6 to 11. A pH of 8.2, for example, supports a plants and fish well, while a pH of 4 (which is acidic enough to dissolve nails) would obviously be a problem.

Test your water with a simple, inexpensive pH kit available at most garden centers or online. Then, as needed, adjust pH levels with special chemicals purchased through water garden suppliers, made specifically to correct water garden pH.

• Chlorine and Chloramines

Chlorine is harmful to both fish and aquatic plants, and is present in nearly all city water. Luckily, it dissipates from water if you let the water sit for 5 to 7 days. Or you can add a special dechlorinator to remove chorine in minutes. Chloramines, which can also be present in water supplies, are also of concern and can kill fish. Contact your local water supplier to ask if chloramines are present. If they are, treat the water with a chloramine remover before adding fish and whenever you add or replace more than 20 percent of the water.

• Oxygen

Fish need well-oxygenated water to sustain life. That's why a fountain or waterfall, which constantly aerates the water, is so helpful. Plants also are a boon to oxygen levels in water, especially submerged plants, as they release oxygen from their foliage.

Water temperature affects oxygen levels. Water that becomes too warm quickly loses oxygen. So guarantee that it stays cool by designing your water garden so that it's large enough and deep enough that it doesn't quickly overheat in the sun. Also site your pool so it gets some shade, particularly in the afternoon. Add floating plants for additional shade in the water.

• Nitrogen, Nitrates, Nitrites, and Ammonia

Even low levels of nitrogen and its related forms—nitrates, nitrites, and ammonia—can be toxic to fish. A primary cause of high nitrogen levels is too many fish. Fish produce a lot of nitrogen-rich waste, so limit their size and numbers. Also use adequate filtering and clean the filters regularly. Include plenty of marginal plants and submerged plants since they filter and oxygenate the water.

Overfeeding fish also contributes to problems because uneaten food breaks down and produces nitrogen-related waste. Signs of high levels of nitrogen include too much algae or fish dying. If you have a concern about the nitrogen levels in you pond, purchase a test kit and test. If needed, treat with special water conditioners made specifically to control nitrogen levels, by cleaning the filters, and by changing out 10 to 20 percent of the water.

The Wonderful World of Water Plants

Water Garden Plant Tips

Water garden plants do more than just look good. All help purify and filter the water. They shade it and keep it cool. They compete with algae and, with your help, have the winning hand. Some also provide food and cover for fish and other garden wildlife.

Water garden plants fall into one of four groups:

• Water lilies and lotuses grow at the bottom of ponds, with long stems growing to the surface with large, flat pad-like leaves and gorgeous flowers on top. They serve most of the same functions as other water garden plants, but their show-stopping beauty, incredible flowers, and fragrance are what really earn them devotees.

• Marginal plants grow in shallow water. Also called bog plants, there are hundreds to choose from, depending on your tastes, climate, and their availability.

• Submerged plants grow mainly underwater. They are a good addition to a pool or pond to add oxygen to the water and provide cover for fish.

• Floating plants simply float on the water surface, their roots dangling below. They spread rapidly in warm weather and shade the pond, preventing algae growth and cooling the water for fish.

Soil Type

Most water garden plants do well in rich, heavy organic soil from your garden, or in compost mixed with garden soil. A little extra clay content is a plus, and some water gardeners like to add sand to allow water to better move through the soil. Regular potting soil is too light and will float away, but you can also purchase potting soil made specifically for aquatic plants.

Once a water garden plant is potted, top the soil with 1 to 2 inches of pea gravel or very small stones. This keeps the soil in place and also helps weight down the pot. It's a good idea to put a stone or two in the bottom of a water garden container to provide ballast to prevent them from tipping or drifting.

Submerged Plants

Submerged plants sometimes are also called oxygenators, and that summarizes their primary role in a water garden. These vital underwater plants may not be obvious to the casual admirer of your water garden, but they are the unsung heroes. During daytime hours when they photosynthesize, they produce oxygen. This additional oxygen is a boon to fish. Also, their trailing foliage and roots provide a place for fish to hide from predators as well as an ideal place to spawn.

Submerged plants also help keep the pool water clear by filtering out nutrients that would otherwise remain in the water and encourage algae growth.

Most submerged plants are grassy-looking plants that aren't especially attractive, but then again, they aren't readily visible either, so it's not a worry. They're available from any water-garden or aquarium supplier.

How many submerged plants to include? One formula is to add 1 submerged plant for every 4 square feet of surface area. But experiment to find out what works best for your water garden.

Most submerged plants do well when in full sun. Most prefer that their crown—the place where the roots meet the stems—is at least a foot or so deep so that most of the foliage is in the water and buoyed upward.

A few submerged plants flower as well, but they are grown almost exclusively for their foliage and ability to improve water quality.

It may be tempting in a small water garden to put soil in the bottom of the pond and grow submerged plants the way it happens in nature. But this method often makes for muddy water. Also, some of these plants can be aggressive and, if they take hold, will overrun a pool or pond.

In all but the deepest water gardens, most submerged plants grow to the surface of the water and float somewhat along the surface of the water. Some gardeners think this looks messy; others like it because it adds interest and another layer of greenery and flowering to their water gardens. If you don't care for this effect, it's easy enough to occasionally cut back your submerged plants by about half throughout the growing season.

Parrot's Feather (Myriophyllum aquaticum)

Mature plant size: ½–2+ feet high and wide

Hardy: Zones 6–11

Bright green, unbranched stems are lined with feathery whorls of leaves (up to 3 inches in diameter!). There is a dwarf, red-stemmed variety, Myriophyllum proserpinacoides, which is gaining popularity because its growth is more compact and manageable. Another compact type is Myriophyllum heterophyllum. A handsome, vigorous plant, parrot's feather is not content to remain underwater and may poke its head out or even trail over your display's edges (or the rim of its container, if you grow it in one). It shelters baby fish, and also does well in deep water pools, so plant it two feet or deeper. In any event, though, you must keep after it, tearing out excess growth so it doesn't overwhelm small pools or entire sections of larger pools.

Parrot's feather is invasive and is banned in Alabama, Connecticut, Maine, Massachusetts, Vermont, and Washington.

Hornwort (Ceratophyllum demersum)

Mature plant size: 1–2 feet high, trailing

Hardy: Zones 6–10

You may have seen this one in aquariums (including plastic versions), and it makes a fine transition to an outdoor water garden.

Once you drop it in the pool, it remains underwater, neither floating on the surface nor sinking right to the bottom—oddly enough, it can exist without developing any roots, though in some situations it will loosely anchor itself to the bottom of a pond. During winter, it drops down to lower depths. It can be used in still or moving water, so it would work in ponds with fountains.

Fish often seek shelter in hornwort's whorls of thin, needle-like, branched foliage, or even spawn within its bounds. Koi tend not to bother it. It makes excellent cover when planted in groups for tiny newly hatched fish to hide in from overhead predators and larger fish that might eat them.

Water Garden Fish

Some homeowners install a pond in their backyard specifically so that they can enjoy fish and other aquatic creatures. Fish in a water feature make it seem more alive and more enchanting. Water features, too, can host other creatures that lend to their interest and diversity, including snails, frogs, toads, butterflies, dragonflies, turtles, birds, and more. Fish have their role in the overall ecosystem of a pond. They can be useful scavengers, nibbling algae and organic debris, including decaying plant stems and foliage. They eat pest insects, particularly mosquito larvae. Last but not least, the carbon dioxide produced by their respiration is immediately available to your plants.

How Many Fishes?

If you put too many fish in your water feature, conditions will become unhealthy due to too much fish waste and too little oxygen. The number of fish you add depends on how large your water feature is, how much filtration you have, and how many plants. A conservative rule of thumb is 1 inch of fish for every 10 gallons of water.

Another rule of thumb, which allows for squeezing in more fish, recommends 1 inch of fish for each 6 to 12 square inches of water surface. For koi, however, double the amount of water surface required.

Aeration also plays a role. If you have a small fountain in your pond, you can have a two or three more fish than if you didn't. If you have a waterfall, which aerates the water substantially, you can have as many as double the amount of fish as you could without a waterfall.

A Good Environment for Fishes

If fish are important to you, design your water feature large enough to accommodate the size and number of fish you want. If you live in a colder climate in the northern two-thirds of the United States, you will need to make some decisions about over-wintering your livestock. This is a complicated issue that you should discuss with the fish seller or other water gardeners in your area.

Different fishes also prefer different depths.

Koi need space to swim vertically, and need at least 2 feet of depth but they are happiest with 5 feet. In comparison, orfes spend most of their time in the upper regions of a pond and are content with very shallow water.

Filtration and aeration are important in features with fish, but be aware that fountains and filtration in a small pond can produce too much churn for fish. Tiny fish can get caught in even modest-sized mechanical filters and a waterfall or fountain may require fish to fight a current more than you would imagine.

Tropical Fish in a Water Garden

Some pond enthusiasts like to put tropical fish—the kind usually reserved for aquariums indoors—in water features. This can be done as long as the weather is warm enough. Most tropical fish don't like water temperatures below 70° F, which means air temperatures that aren't dipping at night below what your house might be like—65° F degrees or so. For the northern two-thirds of the country, that means tropical fish must spend colder parts of the year indoors in an aquarium.

Care and Feeding of Water Garden Fish

Add fish to a pond in late winter or spring when the water temperature has reached around 50°F, roughly your area's average last frost date. Add them only after you are sure your pond is chlorine- or chloramines-free.

Acclimate the fish to the pool by floating the bag in the water for 15 or 20 minutes before releasing them. This allows them to gradually adjust their body temperatures—otherwise, they may die from temperature shock. After putting the fish in the pond, don't feed them for 3 to 4 days.

If you already have other fish, as a safeguard, when introducing fish to a pond with other fish, you may want to treat them with special fish salts to ensure that they are disease- and parasite-free so they don't spread any problems to other fish.

How to Feed Fishes

In a pond with plants, it's easy to overfeed fish. Some may be fine without any feedings from you at all, instead eating plant roots, algae, and mosquito larvae.

Do check once or twice a week, however.

Sprinkle a bit of food on the water. If the fish are not ravenous and do not eat the food immediately, they have plenty of food already. If they do eat well, do not give them more than they can eat in five minutes. Overfeeding contributes to waste in the water and will cloud water and create other quality problems.

Periodically review this list to make sure you are keeping up with summertime chores in your water garden. You'll prevent little problems from becoming big ones.

• As needed, step up the cleaning of mechanical filters. Warmer weather can mean more particles to filter out.

• Expect an algae bloom about two to three weeks after cleaning your pond or once the water reaches warmer temperatures. If it doesn't clear up on its own in a week or two, make sure you're doing everything you can to keep your pond balanced (see pages 16–17), or use an algaecide.

• In mid- to late summer, as needed and if desired, divide marginal plants that are severely potbound.

• If you have newly hatched fish, make sure they have protection from larger fish or other predators that may eat them. Mature submerged plants are ideal for them to hide in.

• As temperatures rise, evaporation increases. Top off the pond regularly, but never add more than 10 percent fresh water at a time or you may kill fish.

• Keep yellowed, damaged, or dead foliage trimmed off water garden plants.

• Fertilize water lilies and other heavy feeders regularly with an aquatic plant fertilizer.

• In summer, with plants and insect populations at their peak, fish may get their nourishment elsewhere. In addition to leaves falling upon your lawn and garden, leaves will also fall into your water feature. Make sure to stay ahead of the leaf fall, preferably every day.

• Skim or rake out leaves from your pond daily or they will break down and encourage algae growth and other problems in the pond. If you have lots of leaves, consider installing a net over the pond or a portion of the pond to catch them.

• If you need to do an overall cleanout of the pond, and plan on keeping it running over the winter, fall is a good time. Fish are strong after summer, and cooler water temperatures keep them more sedate and less likely to be stressed by moving them to clean the pond.

• Determine how you will care for your fish and plants for winter. Stock up, as needed, on grow lights, a de-icer, an oxygen pump, aquarium supplies, and more.

• Keep track of water temperatures (use a specially made water garden thermometer). When temperatures get down to 55° to 50°F, it's time to start preparing your water garden for winter.

HEALTH/MENTAL BENEFITS

Actually, listening to running water is naturally calming. But building a pond also provides a place of sanctuary- a safe relaxing place to escape from the rest of the world. This is one of the many mental health benefits to having a pond. There are other psychological benefits like promoting calmness, focus, creativity, better sleep quality, and something called the blue-mind, coined by Wallace J. Nichols. Water has an effect on the brain to the likes of meditation. It gives you a Zen-like calm feeling, ultimately reducing stress and anxiety. In addition, water, in all forms, releases negatively charged ions into the air, which combats free radicals and purifies the air of dust mites, pollen, germs, allergens and pollutants, and in turn keeps your body healthy. These negative ions are also believed to boost serotonin levels, which relieve stress and depression, and help to increase energy, alertness, and concentration.

- **Financial Incentives**

Ponds can actually be a way to save money. An attractive effect of having a pond is that it can serve as outdoor air conditioning. When water evaporates off the pond's surface, the process reduces heat, which naturally cools the surrounding area. This evaporative cooling is greatly appreciated, especially when temperatures are high and humidity is low, so you can enjoy being outdoors instead of being inside with the AC cranked up high. Your wallet will thank you as well because it will help to keep those electricity bills down. Another benefit to having a pond is to create a natural reservoir if you experience a lower-than-normal season of rainfall. By positioning your drainpipes from your rooftop to empty directly into your pond, you create natural water conservation. Another utilitarian use of ponds is that they provide water storage. Having clean freshwater available in case of an emergency will help bring peace of mind. A well-designed pond can also be a way of dealing with soggy spots or rain runoff in a backyard. The pond also can be used to water plants in your yard during a drought, dry season, or after a frozen winter. Simply dip a watering can into the pond to care for other soil-based plants around your house and yard. All of this water conservation ultimately offers an alternative benefit: lower utility costs, especially in the months with hotter-than-usual temperatures.

• Environmental Benefits

The greatest benefit of all may be how ponds enhance the environment. Not only is water conservation a financial benefit but it helps the environment as well. Gallons of water are used each month in the care of lawns and plants but having a pond cuts down on that water usage. Once a pond is initially filled, it virtually waters itself by re-filling with rainwater. They occasionally need to be topped off or are in need of a partial water change, but ponds rely mostly on natural sources of water to maintain a healthy ecosystem. The moisture provided by a pond can be helpful to nearby plants by offering a self-sustaining cycle of hydration that keeps plants alive without having to water. This helps to maintain soil moisture during the hottest days of summer. And when you build a pond it takes up a nice portion of your yard requiring less mowing, which emits fewer pollutants into the air. This also means fewer pesticides and fertilizers are used for lawn care. These products can be harmful creating toxic runoff that ends up in our water supply. But adding a pond or water garden to your backyard not only can save you money on fertilizer, reduce air pollution, and water toxicity—the sludge collected by your pond filter is a natural fertilizer that can be used to feed your landscape. A major benefit of a pond is that is indirectly supports wildlife that has grown scarce in the suburban parts of the country. Ponds provide sanctuary by offering food, water, shelter, and a place for breeding of indigenous wildlife like dragonflies, frogs, and birds. Include some plants that are native to your area, in and around your pond, as these often provide the best sources of food and cover for native wildlife.

• Education & Interaction

A garden pond and waterfall can provide an area of relaxation while providing interaction and education. Watching as wildlife breed and survive can inspire children and older individuals to find out more about the natural world and their relationship with it. This creates environmental awareness and getting kids involved in the process of planning, building, and maintaining a pond or water garden can help them understand how a complete, natural ecosystem works. It can also help teach children about the responsibility we all have for caring for our environment, which can arouse their interest or passion in creating a better future for our planet.

CONCLUSION

Did you know that ponds have many benefits beyond being a decorative addition to your yard? Adding beauty to your backyard is one of the most obvious benefits of owning a pond. A pond can become the focal point for your garden especially when it includes colorful fish and plants. Additional features such as waterfalls, spitters, statues, or rock borders can be pleasing to the eye as well. Lighting can also set the mood particularly at night.

Close your eyes and listen to the sounds of the ocean, the rain, or running water. In minutes you are instantly relaxed. The sound as water filters into and out of your pond creates the same effect as those mentioned above. The power of the sound of water on the brain is truly amazing. Besides providing a Zen like mood, water creates a form of sound masking. Adding a pond will help to create white noise, especially if you have a water feature like a fountain or waterfall, which will help to cancel out the noise of street traffic or loud neighbors. Point the water feature towards whichever area needs it most, like a bedroom, deck, or kitchen. Having a planted backdrop surrounding the water feature will reflect and focus the sounds of the water.